The art of thi

MIEKE MOSMULLER

THE ART OF THINKING

OCCIDENT • PUBLISHERS

Proofreading:
Sebastian Tombs

Occident Publishers
Post box 306
5110 AH Baarle Nassau
The Netherlands
Phone: 0031 - 13 - 5079948 E-mail: info@occidentpublishers.com
Website: www.occidentpublishers.com

Cover image: Diederik van Leeuwen
Graphic design: Carina van den Bergh

ISBN/EAN: 978-90-75240-481

Contents

Introduction

Pandora

One of the Greek sagas tells about two brother Gods, Prometheus and Epimetheus. They are sons of the generation of the Titans.

In Greek mythology the Gods always have a perfect quality that is their true *being*. Thus Epimetheus exhibits the fully developed quality of having thoughts on the basis of the perception of the senses. He sees, hears, smells, tastes ... and has his thoughts about them. His thoughts thus always follow reality, they are thought after things have happened. Epimetheus can be seen as a being in fully developed, perfect and luxurious surroundings, dreaming his thoughts about all these beautiful things; he can also be seen as smitten by unlucky destiny.

Prometheus, on the other hand, never has his thoughts after things have happened - he has them beforehand. He doesn't live in luxurious surroundings, for all things have first to be created. He is always active, always at work, hardly ever resting. And because of this 'prior-thinking', he has the capacity of prophecy.

Through this capacity he sees that the great Titans will have to step aside to transfer Chronos' reign over the world to the young Zeus. But the Titans won't listen, and wait until they have been defeated. In the meantime Prometheus, with his prophesying, helps Zeus and so becomes his trusted friend. But then Prometheus notices that the human race is withering, and that Zeus is losing his interest in human beings. So Prometheus, who loves humanity, steals fire from heaven and gives it to the human race, so that they can develop themselves further. He also teaches them craftsmanship.

Zeus, of course, is furious about this and he punishes Prometheus by chaining him to the Caucasus, where he will have to suffer forever: during daylight hours an eagle devours his liver, during the night the liver recovers; and so it goes on, in perpetuity.

At the same time, another punishment is hung over the human race. Zeus created a perfect young woman, with the help of all his Gods. Hephaestus created her physical form, Pallas Athena gave her life, and Hermes gave her the power of speech, breath, voice and word. Aphrodite gave her the power of love, the power to seduce...

The other Gods gathered all kinds of good and bad habits in a box, which they gave to the beautiful young lady. Because she now had all the gifts of heaven and hell, she was called Pandora, which means 'all-gifted'.

Prometheus had warned his brother about this Pandora, who he had seen in his prophetic visions. He could tell exactly what would happen, should Pandora come to his brother. He would look at her and without any forethought, he would simply do what Zeus had planned: he would be seduced by Pandora - and he would naïvely open Pandora's box.

So Epimetheus did... And out of the box came, as a kind of

smoke, all the cares, grief, concerns, and troubles that spoil a human life. They whirled about like ungraspable thoughts, ever changing, never quiet, tormenting the human soul forever.

Only one consolation whirled amongst these 'trouble-thoughts'. It didn't vanish; it also remained with humanity: it is hope, hope that things will get better....

So within these two forces, human thought whirls - suffocating on one side, being comforted on the other. Cares, grief, concerns, troubles - and hope.

There seems to be only one power that can be of assistance: it is the power of fore-thought, the power of Prometheus. But he is chained to the Caucasus, suffering from his constantly ravaged liver, pecked at by an eagle....

Thoughts

In ancient times, wisdom was not conveyed in plain thoughts, but clothed in images. These images are not to be understood by our intellect as plain truths. Wisdom is given, but given in pictures. Everyone who is living in our stressful world will recognize the 'gifts' from Pandora's box: cares and troubles - and hopes, all being the subject of our thoughts. Thinking goes on and on, for as long as we live. It even continues when we are sleeping. When we fall asleep or when we wake up, we grasp some snatches of these thoughts when later remembering our dreams.

The moment we recognize that our thinking is never restful or peaceful, we start longing for such rest. Thinking can be beautiful and hopeful, filled with love-thoughts whenever we are daydreaming ... but it can also be tormenting and generate all kinds of stress. Thoughts are, in fact, mostly conscious feelings. First come the feelings, then the thoughts follow, and through thinking we become conscious about these feelings.

Trying to flee from our thoughts is a fruitless undertaking. We can fly to Australia or Tibet or Brazil, and so escape from our everyday circumstances. These everyday thoughts will change, too - but our deeper feelings that are the content of thinking will travel with us, wherever we go. In earlier times it was easier to make a fresh start - for instance during three weeks of vacation - because all the ties to home were broken for a time and our feelings faded away... In modern times we have our what's app, sms and gmail with us - and we never quit thinking in our normal way .

The new forms of social media supply us with thoughts in all corners of the world, and it even can be scary if we have no access to the internet or to some other network. We carry Pandora's Box around with our smartphone in our pocket or our bag; it is a source of happiness, but also a source of worries and troubles of every kind. Thoughts, images, conversations, likes, dislikes, shares ... pop up every minute, just like our thoughts do. Our thoughts guide the use of the 'box', but are also being directed in a way by the box.

We go to a wellness-center, for massage, diet, fitness, sauna, swimming... and the thoughts just keep rolling on, even getting stronger, the more I relax! Maybe they will stop when I have run 40 kilometers, because by then I will be so tired, that my thoughts will only be about my physical feelings and the question of how to reach the finish - but that can hardly be called a relaxation.

So we try to relax - and realize that thoughts never relax. They go on and on, and on - till death ... or maybe they will still go on after death? What a terrible idea...

In Buddhism, Zen-Buddhism, Hinduism, Yoga, and in the western mindfulness programmes, these problems with thinking are well-known. Krishnamurti was an independent teacher for the western people on the basis of eastern principles. He tried to teach us how to recognize thinking as the spring of all disputes, both inner and outer, of all struggles and fights. He recognized thinking as being built up by country of birth, family, education - as a burden that makes it impossible to *live* our lives. His art was guiding the attention to perception and to the recognition that if the perceiver and the perception are one, there can be no dispute, no struggle. His lectures remain wonderful to read, suggesting the possibility of finding rest and peace in our inner lives, by 'taking off our thinking cap'.

Thoughts distract our attention to life, they turn us into beings that are fully absorbed in ourselves - or in the small 'box' in our hand that resembles our outward self; this box seems to have become a thing that bears thoughts, that produces thoughts. We see people walking around with 'thoughts' in their hands, 'thoughts' that are even more difficult to stop than their own thoughts - although the 'box' could be kept unopened ... or could easily be closed.

So what is the use of this book? Another book about finding happiness? If so, then let's just go to the oriental masters or to the courses on mindfulness and yoga.

That thoughts are a source of stress and egoism is clear enough. That it would be very good to find a way to regulate thinking, is also clear enough. But the question is: How do we do that, how do we proceed? And then, what do we achieve by proceeding towards regulating our thinking? That is what this book is all about.

Two directions

When something in life is tormenting us, there are always several ways to cope with it. Take an allergy, for instance: someone is allergic to cow's milk. The advice will usually be to avoid cow's milk completely. The question is whether this consitutes a weakening therapy. Another therapy is the so called desensitisation. The theory is that by giving very small amounts of milk, or injecting a minuscule amount subcutaneously, and then increasing the dose slowly, the patient will start fighting instead of fleeing. He will develop a way to get used to milk. In nutrition we always take in substances that are natural but not human. The living body has the ability to transform these substances so that they become human, so that the human body can use them. Were they to stay purely natural, they would act as a kind of poison and the patient would become ill. In fact, an allergy is a form of inability to transform the substance, and the immune system treats it as a 'corpus alienum', a foreign body, that has to be expelled.

So there are two directions in coping with problems in nutrition: avoid the specific natural substance, accept that you are not able to transform it - and in fact accept your weakness; or try to learn how to transform the natural substance to humanize it. Of course this is not possible by learning systems; we can't be taught how to transform a substance. But we *can* try to get used to it, beginning with 'microscopic' bits.

In psychotherapy this is also well-known in the therapy for fear and fright. The one direction is avoiding all situations that can evoke such fear: avoid all triggers. The opposite direction is to expose patients to small amounts of fear and enable them to become stronger little by little. Or even to try reinforced therapy, that is, to expose patients to very strong fear, to have them 'jump into the deep', and overcome the fear by experiencing it in its worst form.

It can easily be seen that the reinforcement of the patient's inner power will be the strongest in the last therapy, but it is also clear that it is the hardest way - and maybe not always the safest way.

Now let's turn back to thought, to thinking. The rose follows a kind of inborn thought - the rose-thought - and she does that in a perfect way. Only outer circumstances can hinder her, her own way will always be to become a perfect rose. The lion has something else again that he follows in a perfect way. Not only his outer shape is 'lionly', but so is his behavior. We would not think of blaming him for his furious, savage devouring of living animals and, sometimes, even people... His behavior is perfectly lion-like. We can have the conviction that animals can think. But these 'thoughts' are conscious feelings that are instinctive; a lion has no choice to be anything other than a ravenous being, powerful and full of courage.

But a human being is a complicated creature. He has also his form that is human, whether more or less perfect. But the difference with other forms of nature can already be seen when we look at faces. These are so different; so many worlds speak from these faces... And human behaviour? Maybe we could find a typical human behavior, if we said that it had to be moral... But people in general are not only moral. They, too,

18

act out of instinct, like an animal, but they can refine their instincts by intellectual genius which doesn't have to be moral at all. So that is an aspect of human thinking: for example, using the intellect for egoistic purposes or, in a more general way, by inventing weapons.

The rose only wants to be a rose. The human being wants to be something that may not be possible at all, or perhaps strives for something but doesn't want to fight for it, doesn't want to develop himself. The human being has personal feelings and thoughts, that resemble a garden overgrown with weeds, where no gardener ever comes to weed them... "Let it just grow, and act as you are told to by these 'weed-like' feelings and thoughts" - that seems to be a picture of the human being's thinking.

Not only weeds, though, destroy the human garden. It is also a kind of Zoo or, rather, a jungle. It is inhabited by nice and cute animals, but also by lions, panthers, crocodiles and worse - and we don't even know that they are there! Don't we often want to devour each other out of rage or jealousy, and long for a fight? Isn't that deep down in every human soul? How else could war exist between people; guerillas fighting for certain ideas in politics or religion?

Spoiled by the box of Pandora, completely confused, feeling guilty about things that demand no guilt, feeling proud about things that are nothing to be proud of; suffering intensely from the tangle of feelings and thoughts, with allergic reactions to them, because the substances of feeling and thinking are inhuman...

Should we really learn how to take off our thinking cap? Or is there an 'exposure-therapy', a way to recognize our own feelings and thoughts *and to become a Master of Arts of human feeling and thinking - and acting too, in the end -* which would be the true human degree of Magister Artium.

Nature and Spirit

But in which field can we fight and how can it be done? The modern human being, even when basking in luxury, suffers. He suffers from all kind of circumstances, from his destiny, from life. Everything we do and experience transforms itself into feelings, and they transform into thoughts - these thoughts go on relentlessly, even when the event took place hours ago...

We can go to the doctor and ask for pills. "I am depressed... I am nervous... I can't sleep... I'm so frustrated... I feel insufficient... Thoughts bother me... I am overactive... I want to, want to, want to... - and I do nothing at all..." Maybe the doctor prescribes some pills, tranquillizers, anti-depressive medicaments, sleeping pills... The perception of the misery becomes less intense by taking pills – but so also does the perception of happiness, of a fortunate destiny. We don't even notice our happiness any more, and our misery remains, although on a lower perceptive level.

We can go to a shrink and ask for psychotherapy. "I am depressed etcetera...." If the psychotherapist doesn't prescribe pills, he will start another kind of therapy - and we will experience that no-one can do anything about our troubles - except we ourselves. If I have to conquer my fears, I have to do it myself, whichever way I choose. Maybe the shrink understands better what I need, and knows ways that I'm not aware of, to solve my problems. But the way will always be *my way*. Apparently there is some entity in me that can go in a certain direction if I recognize it as the right way.

So what is the right way?

How to achieve rest in feelings and thoughts? The people in the orient have much more restful minds and souls. They have spiritual teachers that have wisdom about reaching this restful state. They have come to the west and have tried to teach us how to uncramp our feelings and thoughts. They have brought yoga, ayurveda, Buddhism, Zen-Buddhism; the Baghwan (Osho) came to Europe, as did the Maharishi with transcendental meditation, and Krishnamurti - and the occidental people longed for this oriental restful state, so they became pupils - and after a while became masters too. They adapted oriental wisdom to occidental approaches - and so, for instance, developed mindfulness practice, and also the spiritual path of the American guru Ken Wilber.

All these teachings point to a state where the human being steps out of his associative thinking where thoughts go on and on, and concentrates on something other than thinking. This may be via the physical training of yoga, the avoiding of intellectual thinking through Zen-Buddhism for instance, the focusing on something other than thoughts through mindfulness, the trying to become conscious of the eternal state of the I, existing beyond life between birth and death, as Ken Wilber and others teach.

The main strategy in all such teachings is actually more or less the same: concentrate on something other than thinking, and let the thoughts simply come and go. They will not harm you any more if you become attentive to other activities.

That is the point of concentrating on breathing. The attention is drawn away from thoughts, and the only perception that is left is respiration, in and out, in and out, let the air imbue your whole body, up to your toes, your fingertips, your deepest organs, your brain.

Or concentrate on a rose... let the rose be the only content of your feeling and thinking, nothing else interests you anymore... Attention is drawn from thinking to the perception of the rose....

So you become used to mere perception, without thinking, without thoughts. You become used to 'taking off your thinking cap'; attentiveness to life's fundamental facts originates here, you become more mindful, without those ever-whirling thoughts....

In Zen-Buddhism we learn to step out of our cognitive answers to questions. To the question: What is Buddha-Nature?, there are many answers. False answers are always the ones trying to explain what the Buddha-Nature is, because these are the cognitive answers. A Zen-Master would slap us hard in the face, or pull our nose were we to give a cognitive answer like that. But if we answered: The Buddha-Nature is the cypress in the garden of the monastery ... it would be a true answer. Quitting cognition is the healing of the soul in a Zen-Buddhistic way.

In transcendental meditation the pupil receives a mantra that is specific for the person, and it has no meaning. One has to concentrate on this specific, meaningless mantra and let it grow thinner and thinner, till eventually it disappears entirely - and an empty consciousness is left.

Following Ken Wilber, I have to learn that the I is the entity that has always been there. Whatever I think, feel, experience in my life, the I is always watching, it is there now, it was there yesterday, it was there for seven years, it was there when I went to school, it was there even when I didn't go to school, it was there when I was born, it was there before I was born, it was there a century before my birth, a thousand centuries etc... It seems to clear up my mind, this going back with my I. But actually I should stop at the first memory. Up to that point I can certainly state that my I was there - but before that I can't say, with my I, that my I was already there, because I lack the experience of my I - I simply don't remember. So here I have to believe what Ken Wilber says, i.e. that I was there also before I knew that I was there. Most people will not go that far in trusting someone: if we speak about the I, we will have to respect the I. That means that we can't ask the I to believe that it was also there when it couldn't yet say 'I'... Before my first memory in childhood, I will have to *presume* that my I was there already.

This example shows us, that we need to *think* if we want to see if a path can ever be *my own path*.

In mindfulness I develop myself by replacing thought with perception with the senses. I draw my attention to the senses. The senses are part of my physical body, they belong to nature. So I turn from thought in my soul to perception with help of my physical nature. Maybe thoughts are also of a physical origin, because they seem to have to do with my brain, but it is less clear to state this. Sure and clear, however, is the statement that my senses are natural and that they are physical organs.

Cure with the analogy, or with the antidote

In medicine, too, we know of two directions in healing illness: we can try to give a medicine that fights against the illness; or we can give something that in nature is working in an analogous way, that works along with the illness and in doing so, cures it. In medicine these two approaches are known as allopathy and homeopathy. Allopathy is the way to fight illness by medicaments in what is now the usual way. It is the medical science that is being taught at university, that is practised in the hospitals and by the medical specialists and general practitioners. It is based on scientific evidence and it therefore has a scientific status.

Homeopathy, however, has no scientific status at all. Although it is also based on trial and error and has a tradition built up over centuries, it continues to be doubted by science, by doctors - and thus also by laymen, by patients.

I don't want to start a discussion here about homeopathy and allopathy. I just want to use the principle of curing things by an analogue instead of by something in opposition, (an antidote) to demonstrate a way of metamorphosing the thinking life by nothing other than by thinking itself.

In the last chapter I spoke about different ways to achieve rest in thought-life, by diverting attention to something other than thinking. Now I would like to show the other way:

getting a restful mind *by* thinking. In this approach, we don't want to conquer thought by 'taking off our thinking cap'; instead, we want to cultivate our thinking so that we become a master in the art of thought. This path constitutes an exposure therapy *and* a homeopathic therapy as well. We will not flee from thinking, but face it as forcefully as possible, and try to transform it - by using thinking itself.

The first exercise, example 1.

We will try to give our train of thought a direction that we ourselves choose. We will not be led by associative thoughts that come and go; we will think with our will only what we *want to think now.*

Therefore I take a book from the bookshelf, without thinking about which - I just take one at random. In my case I took a travel guide to Italy and opened it by pot luck and my eye came across: *Matera, a provincial capital, surrounded by highlands and sassi.*

I looked up on the internet what sassi are: they are cave houses and even a cave church. Now, I make myself a proposal: I will think for a period of five minutes solely about this sentence, I will form my thoughts about what a provincial capital is, what highlands are, what caves are and so on.

Of course I lack knowledge. As soon as I begin to think, I realize this lack of knowledge. I don't even know where Matera lies in Italy. Nonetheless I can think about the questions: What is a capital, what is meant here by 'highlands', what are these cave houses? It makes me curious, and I plan to look it up afterwards; but now I can think for five minutes about everything I *do* know.

26

Matera, Italy

Matera is a city and a province in the region of Basilicata, in southern Italy. It is the capital of the province of Matera and was the capital of Basilicata from 1663 to 1806. The town lies in a small canyon carved out by the Gravina.

Known as "la Città Sotterranea" (the Subterranean City), Matera is well known for its historical center called "Sassi", considered a World Heritage Site by UNESCO since 1993, along with the Park of the Rupestrian Churches.

This is what I found out later; the next time I do the exercise, I will know better what to think about.

First exercise, example 2.

I know a lot about the Logic of Aristotle, so I wouldn't want to select a book of Aristotle to provide me with an exercise in thinking. So I went in another direction, to a cupboard containing none of Aristotle's books - which was itself already a kind of choice. So, without looking, I took down a book from this non-philosophical collection, and I ended up with a book in my hand that was given to me on account of my work about Aristotle! As I opened it, my eye fell on a sentence from ... Aristotle, maybe the most fundamental sentence: *'Substance (ousia) in the most proper, original and excellent sense is the one that is not a predicate of a subject, nor is in a subject, as for instance a certain human being or a certain horse.'*

Although this sentence is very familiar to me, it always poses a kind of challenge to think it over and to try to complete the thought.

If we try this method again and again, taking new content for thinking from time to time, we will discover that the sentences we find in this way are rather suitable for us to think about. We will start to wonder about it, wonder about how it is possible that by simply taking a book from a shelf and opening it, we find such appropriate thoughts, about which we can think for five minutes and give our thoughts the direction we ourselves want to. The first thing, of course, is to understand the meaning of the sentence. That is rather difficult if you don't know the thoughts of Aristotle! But it remains a challenge to think about the meaning, even when you know the sentence very well.

First exercise, example 3.

I took a book from the shelf that turned out to be 'Years of Childhood' by Leo Tolstoy. I read: *The head was Wolodja's first pencil drawing, and on this day - grandmother's name day - it had to be given to her.*

It is a sentence in a novel. We can do all kinds of thinking experiments with a sentence like this. At first we can try to paint an image inwardly of the short scene. But then fantasy carries us away, and we aren't really thinking any more. So I choose the word 'pencil' from the sentence - it could also be 'name-day' or 'grandmother' - and try to think about this object for five minutes, without letting my thoughts drift away.

This first exercise brings *will* into thinking. We don't allow our thoughts simply to go on and on, but we try to think them with will. Five minutes seem to last a lifetime suddenly! We discover that thinking has something to do with time, and that time goes so fast because we don't really form our own thoughts.

There's a kind of richness that we find here. First, the wonder about the finding of sentences that turn out to be very appropriate. Second, the *will in thinking* that makes us find a real filling up of time: seconds, minutes, five minutes... not dreaming for one second, not drifting into sleep.

Everyone who starts with these exercises should find his own sentences - and not use mine.

*

In mindfulness it is usual to set aside twice per day a period of 20 - 30 minutes to do a meditation. In the method I am describing here, this should also become a rhythmic process. Waking up in the morning - or later, if you like that better; before going to bed in the evening, or earlier - we should learn to long for this 20 - 30 minutes' meditation, two times a day. In the exercise described, we spent just 5 minutes. So there is a lot of time left. The first exercise is there to get a hold on thinking, so that it doesn't pass by without our being there in it. Only 5 minutes of exercising two times a day brings forward an increasing control of thinking. Of course, we will not perceive this immediately, it will take some time, maybe a month or so - but then we *will* perceive a strength in thinking that we can sense focused in a point between the eyes, just above the nose. We can feel that we have developed something that would never have been there if we hadn't done this exercise: just 5 minutes, two times every day.

We need this strength to do the next exercises; but we need to continue growing this strength, we don't have to wait till it's completely there...

Spiritual traditions in the West

In our times the impression is that true spiritual development is only to be found in the East, and that in the West there is only a religious tradition, not a spiritual one. But there are, in fact, strong European spiritual traditions. In ancient times the Greeks spoke out of these spiritual Mysteries. Plato is still a spiritual writer. Aristotle, however, transforms this mystery-wisdom in his logic and metaphysics. Subsequently Christianity flows across Europe and becomes an exoteric religion, with its headquarters in Rome. But alongside this an esoteric current develops, on one side based on Platonism, and on the other based on Aristotelianism. The Platonic current culminates in Chartres and flows on a little bit up to the time of Marsilio Ficino in Florence, who translates Plato's complete works. The Aristotelian current becomes powerful during the time of the scholastics, of Albertus Magnus and Thomas Aquinas. Aristotle's logic becomes an instrument for the mind to understand the Bible. At the same time, the catholic saints have their visions of God, of the holy Virgin, they experience religious ecstasy - but the old clairvoyance fades away.

We could say, however, that the true spiritual path of the West is the uncovering of the true being of thinking, of knowledge, of wisdom - and, in finding this true being, the essence of the 'real world' can be found. What we encounter as a disturbing element of egoistic thoughts reveals itself as merely a superficial layer of something that is, in its depths, the true meaning of our existence. In this instance I can only state this; I can't substantiate it in any other way than by appealing to the longings of the reader to find the depth of our existence.

To find this ourselves, we will have to do a further meditation of 15 minutes, two times a day. In these short periods we will develop a completely different thinking. We will discover that there are thoughts that are simply what they are, that we cannot think them over, think them out. We have to let them be - and this actually is the meditation. There is a richness of content that we could draw from, but it is helpful to give examples – here are some:

Second exercise

Before starting with this however, we have to shape our souls so that they are in a sound and pure condition. We take a *rock crystal*, one as beautiful as we can find and study it for five minutes as intensively as we can. We try to discover all its lines and sides, its interior, its substance. Then we close our eyes and try to *be* this crystal ourselves.

Third exercise

Having done this, we now fill our whole thinking with one thought content: *Goodness.*

Do we need explanations for this thought? It should not be a word, it must become a thought. Goodness. We can help by thinking a bit around goodness. But it isn't in fact necessary, for everyone knows exactly what Goodness is.

Then we try not only to *think* goodness, but also to *feel* it, really through and through. Even if we don't want to be good, we know what it would be like to be good. Our feeling knows it also, so it is possible to think with the heart, on goodness.

We try to think and feel goodness without thinking *about* it. We try to be in this goodness as long as possible, maybe for a full minute, perhaps even longer. When we realize that we have fallen out of the thought, we start again - and again and again. If it doesn't work we try to think *about* goodness, find examples in history, in modern times, in our surroundings. Then we try again to stay absorbed in the thought and feeling of goodness. This struggle must go on for five minutes at least.

Then we proceed to the next subject: *Greatness*. We know exactly what this is. If we think about Alexander the Great for instance, we know why he is 'the Great'. And in the eastern language, Sanskrit, the word 'Mahatma' is the word for 'great soul'. That kind of Greatness is meant here. We know what we have to think and we can let it go to the heart, to our feeling also - for 5 more minutes. We don't relate it to ourselves, it is not a matter of questioning our own greatness. Thinking is something purely objective, and after thinking objectively we can soak our feelings with this objective 'greatness'....

It isn't a question about possible existence either. It is not necessary to believe in Goodness and Greatness. We can be doubting whether there are good beings at all, whether there are great beings at all. Even if we are doubters, we can think and feel goodness and greatness. It will be difficult, but not impossible.

The final 5 minutes we spend on the thought: *Eternity*. This

33

also is a thought that everyone knows – whether believing in it or not. We can think 'eternity' and try to feel it afterwards, struggling with it for 5 minutes again.

If we are able to do this work in our inner life of thinking during the course of one week, steadfastly two times a day of a minimum of twenty minutes, we will discover how salutary this is: a new side of thinking begins to arise. This thinking is imbued with *will*, because we are thinking exactly what we want to think - only *one* thought, and nothing else. But it seems to be *alive* too, for it grows.

At first it may only be a word with a limited content, and unusual content for thought. But it develops, the content becomes more explicit and detailed, it can be felt more and more, and the feeling of the thought makes this more significant. After every meditation we feel richer inwardly: three concepts that seem to be worth living for, are growing in our inner life. Goodness, greatness, eternity. And because of our efforts not to *think about these ideas*, but just to think them, the ever-present tendency to judge in our thinking seems to loosen itself; we don't need it anymore. What does it matter whether we believe in goodness, greatness and eternity? We can think them without believing in them at all.

That is the beauty of thinking, that it can be free from our personal convictions. Convictions prove to be something other than thinking. Convictions stick to our everyday self. Thinking has the ability to untie us from ourselves and to lift us up to some world that is not subjective, but at the same time is not merely objective. It is an absolute world, self-contained. Before we started with this kind of meditating we didn't know that a world like this exists. Now we begin to sense that it does exist - and that we belong to this world, even more than to the outer material world. We can feel a kind of *coming home*.

From that moment onwards, we will not have to exercise a self-discipline to continue day after day with this meditation. We will start to long for it, exactly as we look forward to coming home, where everything can be trusted, because this is where we belong, where everything is familiar - in a magnificent way.

Maybe you will answer that you haven't experienced this during a week of meditation, that you had to force yourself to find the time for the exercises. Then it is clear that you didn't give your whole effort, your commitment, your dedication. You were too weak, too distracted, too uninvolved. You will have to press on for another week, encourage yourself, galvanise yourself, rouse your spirits. You are used to sitting in front of your TV, your laptop, your iPhone, expecting everything to come naturally. That no longer works. If you go out to play a sports match of some kind, you know how to energise yourself to such a commitment. Remember this, and stimulate your courage, your joy, your activity...

It is the combination of this self-encouraging, this concentration on one thought *and* the effect of this one thought on your thinking, feeling and will that lead to your metamorphosis.

So watch yourself carefully in meditation, and be alert to what it achieves in you: freedom, the growth of thinking, inner richness. Eternity, greatness, goodness... Feel the courage, the joy, the activity in thinking!

The second week

We use thinking for everything. It seems to develop itself on its own and we are not aware that in the depths of it a wise being lives, who knows exactly *how* to think. When we want to get hold of thinking, we will have to deepen ourselves to this wise human being. Thinking runs on and on, and it unfurls itself. Only in science, art and technical matters it seems to become more active, the thinker has to *do* something. But still, thinking is an unfolding of *content.*

Whatever this wise human being in the depths of the soul really *knows,* works as an activity in thinking life. If we were able to become clearly aware of this thinking-movement - movement actuated by our deepest will - we would be able to handle this thinking, as much an activity in itself as in relation to the forming of content.

We would know better where thoughts have their origin, and we would be able to connect the concepts ever more consciously. They wouldn't take us with them - *we* would be the masters, who could determine our train of thought, while knowing ever more exactly what and how we think.

In the kind of meditation that is provided here, we really try to reach the inner being in the depths of our souls. This being knows all the concepts we are unfolding here, and by unfolding them we can reach this wise being.

So: now we change the contents of our inner work. Each meditation we start again with the exercise of controlling our thinking. But alongside this we try to make a firm decision: to look at our thoughts throughout the day, including when we are absorbed in everyday life. Of course it will not work - it will generate feelings of great powerlessness - but focusing on results has to be overcome. The important thing is the effort we ourselves make to try and achieve what what we set out to do, not achieving perfection. But the fact is that we can achieve a great deal, and we will perceive this, more clearly with every passing week.

We commence our meditation with the five-minute exercise of thinking about a new subject that we have found in a book, or that we have decided to repeat several times.

Then we continue our meditation for about fifteen minutes with three new concepts. These are again concepts that everyone knows, we don't have to think a long time about their meaning. The meaning is clear immediately.

For the first five minutes we try to think: *Power.* Power or might is a force that is well-known, but it is worth while to think this force for a time. In power the human *will* extends to faculties or beings and masters them. Being a capable pianist demands power, being a dictator also requires power. A mason is master of his profession, a saint of his urges, a tamer of wild animals is master over them ... and so forth. We can also try to *feel* power, but here we come into a more risky area, because power is not always *good.* It can be, but it can also induce a very bad kind of feeling. To feel this safely we can think about 'mightiness' instead of power. Here a more divine power is meant and we can try to feel this kind of mightiness - even if we don't believe in a God at all..

The second five minutes have to be filled with one thought: *Wisdom*. This concept, which is also a capacity, is not so easy to think. One has to be a little wise already to be able to think wisdom! But on the other hand, everyone knows immediately what is meant by the word 'wisdom'. That meaning is what we have to think now, and again we will feel how the meaning grows through thinking quietly, without trying to fill up the concept with intelligent thoughts. Just think wisdom, not as a word but as a meaning - and it will grow. We will remember wise persons in history, philosophers, theologians, scientists, but also kings, queens, even emperors, writers, artists and so on - and maybe mothers, fathers, uncles, aunts and so forth... Then we can test how wisdom can be *felt,* again.

The last five minutes will be filled with the thought '*Wish*', in the most general way. We could also say 'will', or want, or desire, or eagerness - or *love*. Love would be the highest, purest form of desire, of will. But it is not only love that has to be thought here, it has to be the eagerness, the desire, which through purification becomes love. In falling in love we have a kind of intermediate state between desire and true love. In this exercise the whole world of desires is meant, and they can be good, but they can also be very bad. So it is the thought of 'want', that we think here, as broadly as possible, to its fullest extent, and we try to feel it as a kind of passion of the soul...

It may be very difficult to concentrate on these concepts without having thoughts about them. Maybe we fall asleep while trying. Then we can strengthen our efforts by connecting the concepts with ourselves as a thinker. In thinking there is usually no tie between the thought and the thinker. The thinker thinks the thought, but it is an abstract thought. If I think the concept of the circle, I am not myself a circle while thinking. Here the thinker and the thought are different things.

In the six concepts we have to work with in meditation, however, it is possible *to be* what we form as a thought. When I form the concept 'goodness', it is possible to bind the thought goodness to myself as the thinker. I can manage to 'be good' while thinking 'goodness'. The meaning of the word becomes endlessly richer and more developed if I experience the connection between thinker and thought. Thought can be realized by this connection. Of course, the human being is only truly good if he is a good person in life - not only in thoughts! But I can really *be* the thought of goodness, greatness, eternity, mightiness, wisdom and fully willed love.

This is a new experience. Never before have I felt myself as a thought, or transformed myself into a true concept. It is a kind of magic that I can feel now. In real life it isn't possible *to be what I want to become*. But in my inner life of thinking it now seems to be possible with, admittedly, only a limited number of concepts. But maybe there are more concepts, perhaps at last it will prove to be possible to transform myself as a thinker in all thoughts that are possible?

I close my meditation with the determination to watch my thoughts all through the day - and to think only valuable thoughts, no nonsense...

The third week

During this week we will develop three more concepts. And we will see later on why it has to be these nine concepts and what the reason is for selecting them in particular.

So now: let's forget the previous concepts, and form new ones. The first is '*Virtue*'. This may not be so easy. Virtue is something old-fashioned, something modern young people don't strive for any more. Rather be full of vices than of virtues! The word, however, has a much more extensive meaning, as illustrated by the word 'virtuous'. Virtue means that one knows how to do something in the best way. An excellent violin-player is known as a 'virtuoso'. This kind of being virtuous is a kind of craft, not only in working with the hands, but in working at higher levels of art and artistry, and in the more moral sphere. It is both having knowledge about how to do things, and also being able to do them.

Of course, virtue is a theme in religion, but we aren't talking about religion here at all. When you see a surgeon at work, doing his work with craft - you can call it a virtue. If you perceive a judge forming his judgment in a justified way, you can also call it a virtue. When you live together with someone who knows the right measure in all spheres of life, you can call this virtue. So virtue is both knowing the right way and *doing* it.

The second concept for this week is *Truth*. In philosophy whole volumes have been written about the right concept of truth, and the content of these has changed over the past centuries. But we can also try not to think the concept through, but just to think it as it reveals itself. At first there may not be much of a meaning, but everyone naturally has a clear notion about what truth in fact is. So we try to forget all our knowledge about the significance of truth and try just to think it. It will give a kind of 'sensation' that is felt as the fundamental significance of 'truth'. Again we will have to tie the thought firmly to our own being, trying to think it with the whole power of our self, of our 'I'. For five minutes living as the truth itself, that is what should be realized. It is a kind of challenge to think some concept without thinking it over - and still think it more intensely than ever before. Becoming the concept, filled up with it through and through, producing it as if it were a birth, but still keeping one with it.

The third concept is *Glory*. This is something that isn't familiar any more. It even seems to be a little bit dangerous to think it, to feel it. Modern young people know it only as a kind of ecstasy, a 'going out of your head', an effect of alcohol, but above all an effect of drugs, of exciting parties. That is not glory, but it appears to be glorious. Now however, we have to think it as a concept, not as a state that has to be reached. In the days when religion was common-place, one still had a notion of Glory. The Glory of the Lord, Gloria in Excelsis Deo... The Gloria was a part of celebration in catholic church, a part of the Mass, put to music by famous composers, for instance the 'Messa di Gloria' of Puccini - wonderful music that you should listen to sometime, on You Tube for instance. But even there the Glory isn't that clear. Glory, magnificence, 'superbness'... A kind of 'crown' on all the concepts encountered over these three weeks.

During these three weeks we have formed the following nine concepts: Goodness, Greatness, Eternity, Might, Wisdom, Love, Virtue, Truth and Glory.

The nine concepts: all that exists.

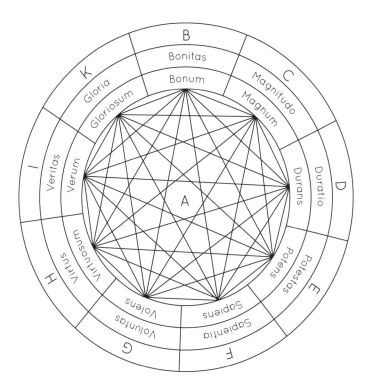

The figure illustrated above came as a revelation to a Spanish luminary and philosopher of the Thirteenth Century: Ramon Lull (Raimundus Lullus).

He developed a system of right thinking that he called 'Ars Generalis', or 'Ars Magna'. Later he wrote an 'Ars Brevis', which is a shorter, more compressed version of the 'Ars Magna'. In this figure our nine concepts are nine parts of a circle: Bonitas = *Goodness*; Magnitudo = *Greatness*; Duratio = *Eternity*; Potestas = *Might*; Sapientia = *Wisdom*; Voluntas = *Will* or Want; Virtus = *Virtue*; Veritas = *Truth*; Gloria = *Glory*. The A in the centre is the being that has all these faculties; for Ramon Lull that was God Himself, centre and periphery.

Now we see how from each point, from each quality, lines are drawn to all other points, to all other qualities. Here we find the opportunity to progress with our meditative thinking, making it more complicated and more differentiated.

We will have to begin at B and then proceed to K. B at first is related only to B. But then a line is drawn to C, then to D etc. This week, we will form the connections within the first three sections; next week in the second three, and the week after in the third set of three. The concepts become richer and richer, until they reach a perfect restful bliss in Glory.

When we think: Goodness, we think about a kind of subject, although it is a quality. When we follow the line to the nearest point, going in a clockwise direction, we can combine goodness and greatness in two ways:

We can say that Goodness is great.

We can say that Greatness is good.

Now we make a meditation out of this. We have learned already not to think in words but in essences. So we think again 'goodness'. But now we add a predicate as an adjective. 'Great' says something about the goodness - and we can try to think this - and feel it again. Good-being is great, we can feel it expand, becoming greater and greater, stretching all over the world, the planets, the stars, maybe beyond the stars.

Don't get bored now, you will discover behind these concepts and their connection the true being of yourself as a thinker.

Then we think again 'greatness'. But now we add as a predicate, as an adjective, 'good'. Good now says something about the greatness, it says that the greatness is good. We can try to think this and feel it again. Being great is good, there is nothing bad in it, it is good in all its greatness. Magnitude. Experience the differences between the connection between the concepts as deeply as you can. Thinking goodness that is great, is very different from thinking greatness that is good.

The most important aspect is the *art of thinking* that can be learned through this meditation. It is not the superficial, ephemeral thinking that we are used to. It becomes more intense with every effort. If we were meditating merely the words, it would be rather ridiculous to do this. It makes sense, however, as soon as we deepen our thinking so that it becomes like feeling the thought, and willing it similarly.

Now we can draw the second line, from goodness to eternity. Goodness is eternal, eternal goodness. Not temporarily, but eternally, actually outside time altogether, where there is 'duration'. A goodness that is not limited by time, neither by a past nor a future, but beyond time.

Then we turn our way back along this line, and duration or eternity becomes the substantive, good becomes the adjective. Eternity is good. Here we should think very clearly and in a differentiated way. Good has nothing to do with the length of time, it is the duration itself that is good, which is rather difficult to imagine. But we can try it over and over again.

The third line is drawn from greatness to duration, from eternity back to greatness, which is a new line. Here we will have to exercise even more effort to think this clearly. To imagine that greatness is eternal is not too difficult. But it is not usual for us to think that eternity is great, without thinking in a quantitative way about endless - 'great'- time. Duration is not time. How can we think the 'ever being' as a 'great' one? 'Great' must be understood here in a non-quantitative way, as we speak about a 'grand dame'. 'Magnificent eternity' could come near to the meaning.

If we try this really as hard as we can, we will soon begin to perceive, that thinking becomes something other than it was before. It arises as an activity capable of making fine distinctions, of seeing fine differentiations, that is increasingly perceived as an inner force.

The fifth week

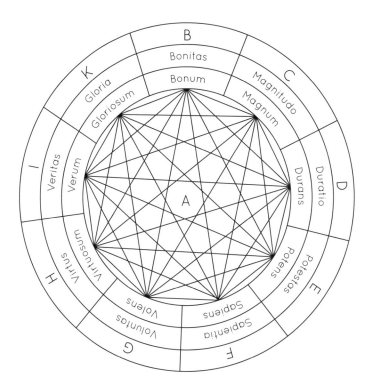

This week we will take the second part of the threefold structure that is set out for us by Ramon Lull. These are the letters E, F and G: Potentas, Sapientia and Voluntas, which can be expressed as '*Might*' or 'Power', 'Knowledge' or '*Wisdom*', and 'Will' or '*Wish*', or '*Love*' in a certain way.

We will be drawing lines again, but now it won't be sufficient to stay within these three concepts. We have to draw a line from E to B, i.e. we say: 'Might is good'. When we have thought this thoroughly and felt it too, we say: 'Goodness is mighty, powerful'. What is important here is the difference between these two combinations, both thought and felt with our whole being. We don't move on to the next three concepts yet, we are staying within six concepts for the moment.

A line is drawn now from E to C, Magnitude. So we think and feel: 'Might is great'; and then vice versa: 'Magnitude is mighty'.

A third line is drawn from E to D. We think and feel 'Might is eternal'. We try to think the reality of a Power that is eternal. Then vice versa: 'Eternity is mighty, powerful'. We can feel by thinking this that eternity could be a full thing, not an empty one. Duration that is full of Might.

Now we turn to the other side: E to F. We think and feel 'Might is wise, a wise Power'. That is something different from being a blind power. Wise power; and then vice versa: 'Knowing is mighty, wisdom is full of power'.

A fourth line goes from E to G and back again. 'Might is full of will'. 'Will is mighty, powerful.'

With every step the process becomes more complex, more vast. Then, when we proceed to point F as the starting point for the lines, we have to begin again, going back to B: 'Wisdom is good', 'Goodness is wise'.

We don't proceed to the fields that we have to yet to reach; we are confining ourselves to B, C, D, E, F and G.

50

For now, I will leave the other lines emanating from F and G for later drawing connections. That is all the work that has to be done in this fifth week! Don't think that it is boring. It may look like that if you don't dive into it. But if you do, you will find the strengthening of your concentrated thinking, the enhancing of your senses, and your faculty of discrimination in complicated matters. Besides, you will become aware that this development of thinking works as a medicine, as a healing activity for your energy, for your body.

The sixth week

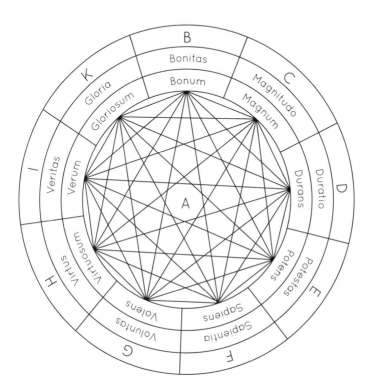

In the sixth week we have to develop our perseverance in thinking even more. First, we always do our opening exercise, the controlling of thinking. Then we do the second exercise, the perceiving and experiencing of the mountain crystal. Then our meditation can start with the third threefold part. H, I and K. *Virtue, Truth and Glory.*

We start with *virtue*. We imagine this concept again, as powerful and light-filled as possible. Then we have to give it six predicates: 'Virtue is good, virtue is great, virtue is mighty, virtue is wise, virtue is full of will'. But it also has to be worked with the other way round: 'goodness is virtuous, greatness is virtuous, eternity is virtuous, might is virtuous, wisdom is virtuous, will is virtuous'.

We proceed to I: Truth. We had thought it already in the third week, and we can now try to think it even more clearly, feel it even more deeply. Then we draw the lines. We can walk along them to and fro individually, we can also walk them all first in one direction and then change the direction - as I suggested for virtue. This is not intended to be a dogmatic system, it is meant to enable thinking with joy, as playing with thinking. It is like discovering a new but well-known world: we discover our home for the first time.

We then take our starting-point at K: Glory. We draw the lines to good, great etc. We have to go around through the whole circle now, which is quite an effort. And we forbid ourselves to just speak the words with their slight meanings. We really *have to* think, which means that we have to take the effort to really think a 'glory that is good ... a goodness that is glorious ... a glory that is great ... a greatness that is glorious'. And so we go on, until the circle closes.

In us arises a beginning understanding of the tree of knowledge.

L'arbre de ciència, 1505.

Intermezzo

The figure and concepts we have been working with are from Ramon Lull, a philosopher and theologian (doctor illuminatus) from Mallorca (1232 - 1316). His '*Ars Magna*' had an influence on many later important thinkers such as Nikolaus Cusanus, Giordano Bruno, Agrippa von Nettesheim, Newton, Leibniz, and Pico della Mirandola. He also had his opponents of course, but that was mostly due to misunderstandings.

Whatever our point of view, we can develop our modern thinking very greatly with the help of this figure with its nine concepts (or rather ten, for A is also a concept, although an unthinkable one). Ramon Lull's most important insight was that human beings can achieve universal understanding between all peoples, between all religions and all political systems - through the art of thinking. Similar ideas are highlighted also in the convictions of Gottfried Wilhelm Leibniz and of Pico della Mirandola.

There was another thinker, in ancient times, who developed ten concepts. And thinking over these ten concepts will form our next step. They are not concepts like goodness, greatness and so on. The concepts that we will be thinking next are the beginning of all logic. We don't have them as fully filled concepts, they are just dynamic forms, by which we can think full reality, not as a complete truth, but as a skeleton for the truth.

This ancient thinker is *Aristotle* and we can draw a new figure, a circle with A in the middle with nine different sections around it. A is the bearer of the other nine concepts.

We can say about a holy person that his goodness is great, eternal, mighty, wise etc. But if there is another holy person beside the first one, we want to note the difference between them. The second also has a great goodness etc. but he is different. This difference lies in A in the new figure. It is the essence of the being, in which all qualities exist, but arranged, composed in a unique way. This is so for holy persons but, of course, also for 'normal' contemporary persons. In such a case the goodness will be less great, or rather small, it will not be eternal and powerful and so on...

How do we distinguish the essence of a being? It is not only human beings that we distinguish in this way, it is also things, facts and processes.

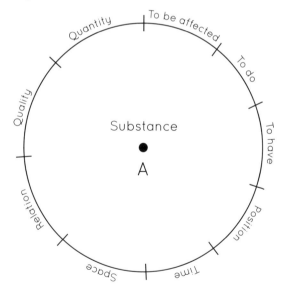

The direction could also be read anti-clockwise, because Aristotle gave the following sequence:

Quantity, Quality, Relation, Space, Time, Position, To have, To do, To be affected. We will, again, have to try it in all possible ways...

The seventh week

Now we will start again with forming concepts, and we will discover the enormous difference between the concepts of Ramon Lull and Aristotle, to find in conclusion how they come together in a kind of musical harmony in thinking.

We start our meditation again with the controlling of thought, then with the perceiving of a mountain crystal.

The first concept is '*quantity*'. If we read what Aristotle has written about this, we find a vast chapter with all possible elements of quantity, such as 'number, measure, weight, amount, bigger, smaller, heavier, lighter, continuous quantity, discrete quantity' and so on.

We will not read Aristotle, however. We know very well what is generally meant by '*quantity*' and we try to think this concept in the same way as we have thought the nine concepts of Lull. We experience that we can't just imbue ourselves with the concept, we actually have to form it first - that is a difference from our thought-action previously. It really must be thought over, even when we don't start to specify it. We can make a quick round of our former concepts and ask ourselves if goodness can be measured quantitatively, if greatness can, and so on. Can these concepts be expressed in a number that has been measured exactly? We will feel that it is not possible, that exact quantity is not a concept that can be used in this field of human existence.

The second concept is '*quality*'. Here again, Aristotle has worked out the whole extent of the possible meanings of quality. But we know the meaning of quality, it is clear to everyone. We must only remove the meaning of all common associations and everyday usage. Quality doesn't say anything about good or bad, it just describes the nature of something or someone. We can also compare the notion 'quantity' with the notion 'quality', and discover the totally different meanings of these two concepts. When we go round the circle linking quality to goodness etc... we will find that these nine concepts are all qualities of a certain high psychological level.

The third concept is '*relation*', in its most extensive meaning. Relatives have a relation to each other, but so do lovers, too. We can compare quantities and qualities and so find relational concepts as: 'different, the same and opposite; beginning; underway; and with an aim or objective; bigger, smaller and equal. But cause and effect also are relational concepts. Then we come back to the extent of the concept, we must learn to think it all at once, encompassing the whole meaning of it, and imbuing ourselves with it. Then we go round the circle again, and we find that we can compare the goodness, greatness etc. of two beings; we also can try to compare the different concepts of the Ramon-circle, so we try to bring goodness into a relation to greatness - and we find ourselves taken back to the fourth, fifth and sixth week of our exercising. We will find the relation between the nine concepts: for instance, that wisdom is not possible without truth, or that virtue is not possible without love. But we still have to go deep into these thoughts, in order that the meditation is not reduced merely to a kind of fulfilling duty without commitment.

The first day will be a great challenge. But over the following days our thinking will become more smooth, clear and, at the same time, deepened. We can learn to live with the concepts as we live with beloved friends, being happy to come nearer to them, to get acquainted with them. We have an intimate relation to them and we will discover that they are our own, that they are inborn.

Goodness we will have to *develop*, if we want to be good. But these Aristotelian concepts live in us as 'judging tools'. These are experiences that we will gain for sure through these meditations.

But then we will have to try to differentiate deeply what we have found in relation to the nine former concepts: try to *feel*, to experience, how quantity cannot be used there, how all nine concepts themselves are qualities, how they can be brought into relation with each other and how one quality can be brought into relation with two different subjects that have these qualities.

We are not used to this kind of thinking. Thoughts are mostly words with slight meanings, coming and going. Now they have to become living beings with their own way of acting. These actions and activities we will have to discover and to experience.

There is a possibility to *hear* a form of this thinking, you can listen to it in music. Actually, all music is *living thought* that can be heard in harmonies and disharmonies. But once there lived a composer, whose thinking was so pure and complex that he could bring it into a musical form. This composer was *Johann Sebastian Bach*. The composition that comes close to the kind of thinking that we are developing here is his *Art of Fugue*. It is written as a kind of doctrine, and it can be played on the clavichord or the piano. But it can also be heard in instrumental and even orchestral performances. The most intensive way of listening to this music - which can never be background music - is to listen to it with the full score along with it, so that you can see the impressive complexity of harmonies in four voices. This can be found on 'You Tube' .

The eighth week

When in the first seven weeks the exercises have been done thoroughly, the inner force and power will be strengthened so much that thinking has achieved some living force in it. What would otherwise be boring and impracticable without these former exercises, becomes an intriguing activity. This inner guide to thinking is not a book you can just read - it would be like a reading a list of words. The reader has to *actively* think!

Now we start the eighth week with three new concepts. First, we do the preparatory exercises, then we form three new concepts.

We think the fourth concept: *'space'*. Again we will have to think this in as extensive a way as possible. But it is not mathematical, physical or philosophical ideas that we need here. We need the self-evident meanings of 'space'. We can think it as an image, not only a cosmic space is space. Space can also be thought in a figurative way, we also have inner space, in our feelings, in thoughts (freedom of thinking or dogmatic thinking), and so on. So we can find a self-evident meaning of 'space' in general. This is what we try to think for about five minutes, not forming ideas, but trying to imbue ourselves with this actual thought.

Then we think the fifth concept *'time'*. In philosophy and in physics the real existence of time sometimes is denied. It is seen as a kind of division of the naturally changing relationship between sun and earth, not as an element with its own true existence. Maybe you, reader, also deny that time is something real. That doesn't matter, for we can think also what we don't believe. The task at hand is to think time as a self-evident reality, in as extensive a way as is possible and not only as the ticking of a clock, but also as something that we have in our inner psychic life, in physiological rhythms (think of the female rhythm of ovulation etc.), in spending time in thoughts, feelings, actions. The feeling for time, the feeling of having time enough, or of being in a hurry. Imbue your whole human being with 'time'.

The sixth concept is '*position*'. This is also a concept that has outer and inner meanings. Aristotle describes this as 'sitting, standing, lying, hanging'. These positions can also be thought in a figurative way. I have a hangover - something bad hangs in the air. Standing also means position, status. A sitting can also describe a period when one performs a certain activity. So we can try to think 'position' as extensively as possible, literally and physically, but also figuratively. In Buddhist tradition there is a state wherein the pupil must exercise 'the right position'. This is the right relation between inner and outer life, finding a kind of balance point between them. We can also think it as a standpoint, a point of view; that also is a position.

But after thinking these three concepts, we will have to do the work of combining these concepts with our first nine concepts. 'Is goodness spatial? Is space good? Is greatness spatial? Is space great?' And so on. 'Has glory a relation to time? Is time glorious?' We have to walk the round again and try to experience what they 'have' with our new concepts. It is not important that we find sure and right answers. It is the vast activity in thinking that matters. And by being that active, we will certainly feel some distinct meanings now and then, feel another 'fugue' and its 'counterpoint', experience the *life* of the different concepts and their connections or disconnections. We don't have to spend much time on these rounds - we can turn it in less than a minute - and feel what happens.

The ninth week

During this week we will form a further three concepts, and in the following week the bearer of these concepts will become the subject for our thinking: substance or being.

I assume that the preliminary exercises - the controlling of thinking and the mountain crystal - have become a habit now. These small exercises will come first before each meditation.

The seventh Aristotelian concept is *to have*, more limited 'to own'. Aristotle describes very briefly what is meant with this category: he means really to have something, but gives the example that 'having' can be used in a false way, for instance when we say: I have a wife. It is false, because a human being should not have another human being as a property. We don't *own* our partner... But we can also think this concept more extensively, in a *figurative way* again. We also 'have' qualities, dispositions, features etc. And material things also 'have' all kinds of qualities and features. Processes - the weather for instance - can also partly be characterized by having certain aspects. The wind 'has' a quantitative power. Then we imbue ourselves with this thought: 'to have'. - This concept provides a challenge: to think the difference between having and being. Finally, we think around our first circle of nine concepts again: 'to have goodness, greatness etc. Goodness has greatness, power, wisdom? Glory has wisdom, truth?'

The eighth concept is *'to do'*, or *activity*: Peter is running, Joan is studying. But here the more extensive way of thinking is also asked for. Not only physical activity should be thought of, but also psychical, mental activity. The work that we do in this meditation certainly is *'doing something'*. Learning a language is activity, interviewing a patient is activity, answering the questions of the doctor is activity. But an avalanche of stones from a mountaintop is not an activity, that has to be ranged in the category 'passivity'. Even the cause of the avalanche can be a passive cause - although somewhere there should be found an activity that is causal. Can material, physical causes, mechanical causes ever be ranged in the category 'to do'? Try to discern this carefully - and feel the difference between an action of a living being as a cause and the working of a physical cause. - Then we imagine the full meaning of 'activity' and imbue ourselves with this meaning. Finally, again, we have to make the round: 'Is goodness an activity, is activity good etc.?'

The ninth concept and the last in this set, is *'affection'*, *'to be affected'* or 'undergoing'. Aristotle speaks about 'being affected'. We can imagine all kinds of sufferings, they always are 'impositions', one has to undergo them. But if a little child wears boots, this also is something passive, a booted child... And we can think this in its full extent: for there are many psychic sufferings. And in philosophy perception with the senses is called a passive phenomenon, in the same way as conceiving thoughts. That would seem to be in contradiction to the sentences in the former paragraph. But here we can conceive the difference between thinking as an activity - in meditation - and thinking as a passive receiving of thoughts. - We imagine the full meaning of 'passive', to its full extent, and imbue ourselves with the thought. Finally we make the round about the circle: 'Is goodness passive? Is passivity good?

Is passion good? Is virtue possible in passivity, can we undergo it? Is passivity a virtue?' And so on and on - but in just a minute or so. Feel the differences!

The tenth week

Now we will have to form a fundamental concept, to which all other concepts are related. Aristotle said it firmly: 'If there were no substance, the other categories wouldn't exist either.' In the figure of Lull we could say: If there were no A, there wouldn't be B etc. either.' Qualities have to have 'someone' that has them. Of course we could try to imagine that the nine concepts are beings themselves - that would be a Platonic point of view. But here we don't want to embark on difficult thoughts that are not so easy to grasp. We want to develop a clear, conscious and just thinking, a pure intelligent thinking that has its foundation in itself. So we follow Aristotle, the founder of logic, with his systematic description of the 'technique' of thinking.

I will give an example of *substance* - a subject - with all its predicates. I quote Wikipedia:

'Aristotle, Greek: Ἀριστοτέλης [aristotélɛːs], *Aristotélēs*; 384–322 BC) was a Greek philosopher and scientist born in the city of Stagira, Chalkidice, on the northern periphery of Classical Greece. His father, Nicomachus, died when Aristotle was a child, whereafter Proxenus of Atarneus became his guardian. At eighteen, he joined Plato's Academy in Athens and remained there until the age of thirty-seven (c. 347 BC). His writings cover many subjects – including physics, biology, zoology, metaphysics, logic, ethics, aesthetics, poetry, theatre, music, rhetoric, linguistics, politics and government – and constitute the first comprehensive system of Western philosophy. Shortly after Plato died, Aristotle left Athens and, at the request of Philip of Macedon, tutored Alexander the Great starting from 343 BC.https://en.wikipedia.org/wiki/Aristotle According to the *Encyclopædia Britannica*, 'Aristotle was the first genuine scientist in history ... [and] every scientist is in his debt.'

'Teaching Alexander the Great gave Aristotle many opportunities and an abundance of supplies. He established a library in the Lyceum which aided in the production of many of his hundreds of books. The fact that Aristotle was a pupil of Plato contributed to his former views of Platonism but, following Plato's death, Aristotle immersed himself in empirical studies and shifted from Platonism to empiricism. He believed all peoples' concepts and all of their knowledge was ultimately based on perception. Aristotle's views on natural sciences represent the groundwork underlying many of his works.

'Aristotle's views on physical science profoundly shaped medieval scholarship. Their influence extended into the Renaissance and were not replaced systematically until the Enlightenment and theories such as classical mechanics. Some of Aristotle's zoological observations, such as on the hectocotyl (reproductive) arm of the octopus, were not confirmed or refuted until the 19th Century. His works contain the earliest known formal study of logic, which was incorporated in the late 19th Century into modern formal logic.

'In metaphysics, Aristotelianism profoundly influenced Judeo-Islamic philosophical and theological thought during the Middle Ages and continues to influence Christian theology, especially the scholastic tradition of the Catholic Church. Aristotle was well known among medieval Muslim intellectuals and revered as «The First Teacher» (Arabic: المعلم الأول).

'His ethics, though always influential, gained renewed interest with the modern advent of virtue ethics. All aspects of Aristotle's philosophy continue to be the object of active academic study today. Though Aristotle wrote many elegant treatises and dialogues – Cicero described his literary style as «a river of gold» – it is thought that only around a third of his original output has survived.'

Aristotle is the subject of this description. Let us try now to think about this individuality, and try to realise that this is what is called: *Ousia*. This is a specialised being, not a being in general, but a being that cannot be further divided: it is the individual. This includes not only a human being or a living being.; it can also be a thing, a table or a tree. But then it has to be *this* table, here or there, at this moment, in this shape, made from this particular material etc. So not 'table' in general, as a general concept.

Here we have a human being, Aristotle. He is no longer living, but lived in ancient times *(time)*, he was born in Stagira, lived in several places *(space)*. He was a philosopher and a scientist (*quality)*. Then follows a description of all kinds of relationships that he had, being the son of Nicomachus; thereafter he had a guardian, joined the Academy in Athens, became the teacher of Alexander the Great, and so on. All these predicates belong to the category of '*relation*'. The 'medium' through which the subject predicates its specific qualities is the category of '*to have*'. It is a binding of something between the subject and its qualities. His working *(activity)* is quite something else. We find it described in the fact that he became an empiricist, in the fact that he practised philosophy and science and so forth, in the fact that he had a deep influence on his contemporaries, which also endured into the middle-ages and even into modern times.

The concepts 'quantity', 'position', and 'passivity', can also be found in this description. *Quantity* for instance lies in the number of years, but also in the number of writings - although these are not known exactly.

Position: "Aristotle was the first genuine scientist in history ... [and] every scientist is in his debt." This is a form of position. We can try to feel other kinds of 'position' in the text.

'*Undergoing*' or 'passivity' lies - as well as activity - in the whole work of Aristotle; it his 'receiving', the way he himself described the human process of knowing as a receiving process. Indeed, the perception with the senses must be conceived as a receiving process.

So we have found the *nine categories* in this description, but the tenth, or the first, is indescribable. All the predicates give some information about this individuality, about this 'entelechy', about the central being that embodies all these qualities etc. But we cannot describe this 'substance', we can only give a paraphrase. Nonetheless every human being has the faculty to perceive this indescribable being, this individuality.

So this is what we have to do in the tenth week: we form images of individual beings, living and material, and try to perceive the being within them, which cannot be further divided without losing its 'substance'. A wooden table that is sawn into two pieces is not the original substance anymore, it has lost its 'substance'.

This is the most difficult concept to think, and the most important one – because, without 'substance', the other concepts cannot themselves exist.

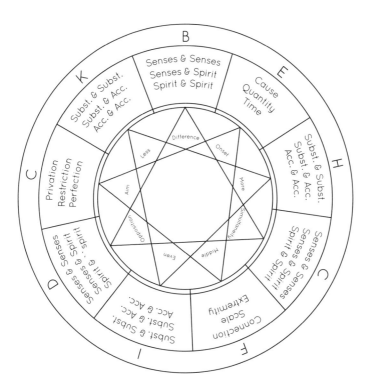

This week we turn back to Ramon Lull, to another figure he has given us in his 'Ars Brevis'. This is a challenging figure. It uses the Aristotelian concepts, but it uses them in a kind of organized way. We see here three triangles and find nine 'star-points' that give us nine new concepts. They point to nine fields that indicate the fields where they work. It becomes rather complicated now, and we wouldn't be able to continue, if we had not developed such strong thinking power over the last ten weeks. The nine top lines identify concepts that have to do with possible *varieties of the category 'relation'.*

In this eleventh week we will take the first triangle that points to B, C and D. In B we find the first concept: 'Difference' (B).

We know exactly what it means. For five minutes we now think this meaning, *without thinking* it over, just concentrated thinking about *'difference'.* Then we allow ourselves to let 'difference' go around our first circle of goodness, etc. That goodness is different from greatness is evident. But goodness can be different in different substances: one person is different in goodness from another person. We can also make a circle along the Aristotelian categories: 'different quantity, different quality, different relation etc.' It is the category *'relation'* that is now making music with the other categories.

Difference plays a role in different sense-perceptible items; in the difference between a sense-perceptible item and an invisible (spiritual) item; or in the difference between two invisible items. This is drawn by Lull in the middle ring of text.

The second concept: *'Conformity, similarity'* (C).

We know exactly what this is, it is a self-evident concept, and we can think it in a concentrated way, imbue ourselves again with the meaning - and then walk around the circle of qualities again: Goodness etc. Walking around the categories: similar quantity, similar quality, same place, same time etc.

Conformity plays a role in similar sense-perceptible items; in the conformity between a sense-perceptible item and an invisible (spiritual) item; or in the conformity between two invisible items.

The third concept is '*Opposition*, contrast, contrariness' (D).

This also is self-evident. After thinking it without thinking it over, we can again think this in relation to the nine concepts and this will be very interesting: 'goodness - badness; greatness - smallness; eternity - temporality; might - impotence; wisdom - ignorance; love - hate; virtue - vice; truth - untruth, error, lie; glory - insignificance, lowliness.' And then the second round: 'contrary quantity, contrary quality, contrary place?' (this seems to be not thinkable), just like 'contrary time,' etc.

Opposition plays a role in opposite sense-perceptible items; in the contrast between a sense-perceptible item and an invisible (spiritual) item; or in the contrast between two invisible items.

Our thinking has now become rather complicated and extended. But there still is no case of a developed logic in thinking. We are still developing concepts. These are the 'finger exercises', the 'scale studies'; it isn't music yet. That has yet to come...

But already our thinking is complicated. We have to think in clear notions and combine them with more complicated notions. And we have to think them without words, because this is a conceptual thinking, not a spoken thinking that we are developing.

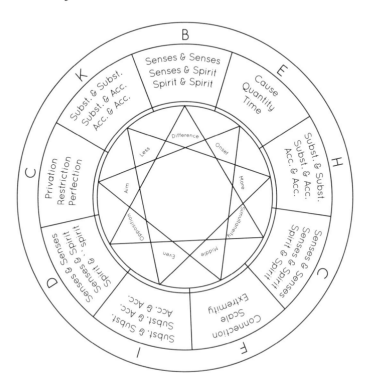

The second triangle points to E, F and G.

We start with Point E as our first concept: it is '*Beginning*', or 'Onset', or 'Start'. With eternity this is incompatible. We can think 'Beginning', we all know what it means. We try to develop a feeling for it, a kind of inner image of a process that has a beginning. We have been training ourselves in the meantime, to think without speaking a word in our mind, and yet still think the full extent of the concept. 'Beginning'.

We can think the *beginning* of goodness, greatness, power, wisdom, love, virtue, truth, glory. We can try to find the connection between '*beginning*' and the ten Aristotelian concepts. This apex points to a region where we can find the three fields on which this concept can be thought: The beginning can have *a cause* (what is the cause of the beginning of wisdom?); it can require a certain *quantity* (with what quantity/level of intelligence can a pupil begin at high school?); it can have a starting point at a certain time (at what age can a child go to school?).

The second concept is '*Middle*', point F. It lies between the beginning and the aim, the end. We can again think this immediately, as a kind of image, a middle between start and end. But it is not meant only as the middle of time/period. It can also be the middle of a process.

'Middle' can be meant as an *intermediary*, a mediation, an interposition, that is the first concept we find above the triangle-top, in the second layer; 'Middle' also can be meant as a *measure*, a size; and Middle can be the middle between *extremities*.

The third concept, in point G, is '*purpose*, aim, intention, goal, end'. If we grasp this in as clear a way as possible, as something that has to be achieved, small or great, divine, human or animal, we can feel it again and perceive it in a kind of imagination, an image. Something that lies at the end of a process, that was aimed for, that had a beginning and a middle point. Now it strives to the end, and a *divergence* can lead to the impossibility of reaching the aim. The other connection is that there can be a *restriction* of the aim, that it can be reached only partly, that the goal is reached in a limited way. And the third possibility is that the aim is fully reached - that is *perfection*.

At the end of each meditation this week we have to play for a little while with these three concepts and their connections. We can also try to find connections to the first and second circles. We need to remember the music, while doing this. Thinking really has an accordance to music. There are seven or twelve 'concepts' there, and there are also two times twelve keys, as we can see in this circle of fifths.

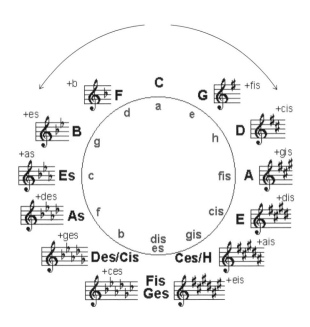

In music, composition is based in one of these keys, and can also modulate to another. Within any key there is a wonderful combination of tones, harmonies, disharmonies and harmonies again. This is exactly in accordance to thinking, as we have exercised it during this twelfth week.

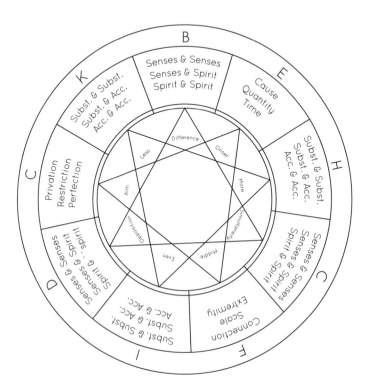

Now we proceed to the points H, I and K. These relational concepts are questioned by Aristotle in all his categories. He always asks whether in this category more, less or the same is possible. As regards *quantity* this seems to be evident. But precisely here it doesn't work: five can never be more five than another five. In position, for instance in the position 'standing', this also cannot be said, one stands or one stands not.

Lull advises us to compare always the substance with the substance: this table looks more like a table than that table; to compare the quality, quantity etc.: e.g. this colour is a more intense white than that; and to compare substance and predicate: this table is larger than that table.

Can goodness be more, less or even? Can eternity be more eternity, or less eternity?

At first we think the three concepts one for one, in as intense a way as possible. It is difficult, exactly because it is so simple. More, less or even.

Then we try to find whether they have *validity* in the Aristotelian concepts. After that, we do the same with the nine concepts of our first figure.

We have accomplished a vast effort of thinking by now. We have learned to think concentratedly, to bring motion in our thoughts, to harmonize thoughts with each other.

Now, in this thirteenth week we can make a significant gesture. We have thought many concepts and have learned a little of the music of thinking. This music cannot be heard with ears, but it can be felt. We feel it already, although we have no clear consciousness of it. We do our exercise of this week, and then we try *to become aware that we are thinking*. It is not the content now that fascinates us, it is *the thinking movement itself*. We can feel it as a strong point in our forehead, a point that is *forceful*, but that also has movement around it, as if we were sailing on the waves of our intense thinking. When sailing on the sea-waves we are on waves that have different shape and speed, but they all have the same meaning: wave-being. In sailing on the thought waves, however, we acknowledge that it is our own activity that generates the motion and that this motion is meaningful: it is filled with the concepts that we form.

Maybe we are used to paragliding, skiing, climbing mountains... at such times we experience something that is far more breathtaking than whatever we have experienced in life. We feel the motion of thinking and we are on it, sailing in a fast glide, sailing away from the trusted stationary thinking to a *free geometry*, imbued with meaning.

In my experience there is nothing on earth that can be compared with this blissful experience - not a temporary bliss, dependent on causes we cannot see - that can be evoked by this form of thinking meditation. It is the foundation for other inner experiences that will be discussed in a second volume.

In this book, we will now have to expand our conceptual thinking into a *thinking of the truth*.

The fourteenth week

Aristotle 'On interpretation'

Part 1

'First we must define the terms 'noun' and 'verb', then the terms 'denial' and 'affirmation', then 'proposition' and 'sentence.'

'Spoken words are the symbols of mental experience and written words are the symbols of spoken words. Just as all men have not the same writing, so all men have not the same speech sounds, but the mental experiences, which these directly symbolize, are the same for all, as also are those things of which our experiences are the images. This matter has, however, been discussed in my treatise about the soul, for it belongs to an investigation distinct from that which lies before us.

'As there are in the mind thoughts which do not involve truth or falsity, and also those which must be either *true* or *false*, so it is in speech. For truth and falsity imply combination and separation. Nouns and verbs, provided nothing is added, are like thoughts without combination or separation; 'man' and 'white', as isolated terms, are not yet either true or false. In proof of this, consider the word 'goat-stag.' It has significance, but there is no truth or falsity about it, unless *is* or *is not* is added, either in the present or in some other sense.

Part 2

'By a noun we mean a sound significant by convention, which
has no reference to time, and of which no part is significant apart
from the rest. In the noun 'Fairsteed,' the part 'steed' has no significance in and by itself, as in the phrase 'fair steed.' Yet there is a
difference between simple and composite nouns; for in the former
the part is in no way significant, in the latter it contributes to the
meaning of the whole, although it has not an independent meaning. Thus in the word 'pirate-boat' the word 'boat' has no meaning
except as part of the whole word.

'The limitation 'by convention' was introduced because nothing
is by nature a noun or name - it is only so when it becomes a sym-
bol; inarticulate sounds, such as those which brutes produce, are
significant, yet none of these constitutes a noun.

'The expression 'not-man' is not a noun. There is indeed no recognized term by which we may denote such an expression, for it is
not a sentence or a denial. Let it then be called an indefinite noun.

'The expressions 'of Philo', 'to Philo', and so on, constitute not
nouns, but cases of a noun. The definition of these cases of a noun is
in other respects the same as that of the noun proper, but, when coupled with 'is', 'was', or 'will be', they do not, as they are, form a proposition either true or false, and this the noun proper always does, under
these conditions. Take the words 'of Philo is' or 'of Philo is not'; these
words do not, as they stand, form either a true or a false proposition.

Part 3

'A verb is that which, in addition to its proper meaning, carries
with it the notion of time. No part of it has any independent
meaning, and it is a sign of something said of something else.

90

'I will explain what I mean by saying that it carries with it the notion of time. 'Health' is a noun, but 'is healthy' is a verb; for besides its proper meaning it indicates the present existence of the state in question.

'Moreover, a verb is always a sign of something said of something else, i.e. of something either predicable of or present in some other thing.

'Such expressions as 'is not-healthy', 'is not ill', I do not describe as verbs; for though they carry the additional note of time, and always form a predicate, there is no specified name for this variety; but let them be called indefinite verbs, since they apply equally well to that which exists and to that which does not.

'Similarly 'he was healthy', 'he will be healthy', are not verbs, but tenses of a verb; the difference lies in the fact that the verb indicates present time, while the tenses of the verb indicate those times which lie outside the present.

'Verbs in and by themselves are substantival and have significance, for he who uses such expressions arrests the hearer's mind, and fixes his attention; but they do not, as they stand, express any judgement, either positive or negative. For neither are 'to be' and 'not to be' the participle 'being' significant of any fact, unless something is added; for they do not themselves indicate anything, but imply a copulation, of which we cannot form a conception apart from the things coupled.

Part 4

'A sentence is a significant portion of speech, some parts of which have an independent meaning, that is to say, as an utterance, though not as the expression of any positive judgement. Let

91

me explain. The word 'human' has meaning, but does not constitute a proposition, either positive or negative. It is only when other words are added that the whole will form an affirmation or denial. But if we separate one syllable of the word 'human' from the other, it has no meaning; similarly in the word 'mouse', the part 'ouse' has no meaning in itself, but is merely a sound. In composite words, indeed, the parts contribute to the meaning of the whole; yet, as has been pointed out, they have not an independent meaning.

'Every sentence has meaning, not as being the natural means by which a physical faculty is realized, but, as we have said, by convention. Yet every sentence is not a proposition; only such are propositions as have in them either truth or falsity. Thus a prayer is a sentence, but is neither true nor false.

'Let us therefore dismiss all other types of sentence but the proposition, for this last concerns our present inquiry, whereas the investigation of the others belongs rather to the study of rhetoric or of poetry.'

In this quote Aristotle gives the foundation of how concepts and words can be thought and spoken without any question about truth or untruth. There is a whole range in thinking and speaking that has not the pain of troubling about truth. In the past thirteen weeks we have been developing this kind of thinking. Now, in the fourteenth week we will have to form the concept of a thinking and speaking that has *no judgment, no proposition* in it - just as we have been practising it in the past weeks.

As always, we first do our exercise with the controlling of thinking. Then we try to become restful in our mind by meditating on the mountain crystal.

For the next fifteen minutes we have to think over the recognition of the existence of nouns and verbs in our thinking, what they are and how they *don't represent truth or untruth as long as they stand alone*, or when they are combined in sentences that make no propositions – for example as in a prayer.

We can go round the first figure once more and find that goodness is not true or false in itself. It becomes only part of truth or falsity as soon as it is connected with a subject to a proposition: 'Napoleon was a good man'. Being good is a verb, is an activity. Was Napoleon a man who was being good? 'Napoleon was a great man'. Was Napoleon a man who was being great? We should pass through all nine concepts.

'Thy will be done.' A sentence from the Lord's Prayer. Here we cannot speak of truth or untruth, because we are praying for it.

Then we pass through the ten Aristotelian categories and try not only to think them in their being verbs or nouns, but also *to experience* this thinking activity, so that the being of the several categories becomes ever more clear and differentiated - as if they were friends, as I have said before.

Difference, similarity, opposite. These concepts have their clear meaning, but in themselves there is no question about truth or not. This will only make sense once a proposition is made: 'This colour is exactly the same as that one there.' 'No, there is a slight difference.'

We will have to clear our mind and think this over and over again, although it may seem uninteresting evidence, or an irrefutability. The evident meanings rest on the foundation of our thinking, it is true, but to raise them into full consciousness is *very significant*.

After fifteen minutes working hard on this theme, we will now make it a habit to take notice of our thinking movement, the great *meaningful* weaving of thought, initiated by me as the thinker.

The fifteenth week

Here, I quote Aristotle again. You don't have to read it if it frustrates you…. You can also go on with this meditation without reading Aristotle. It is meant as an illustration that could help, though.

Aristotle, Part 5

'The first class of simple propositions is the simple affirmation, the next, the simple denial; all others are only one by conjunction.

Every proposition must contain a verb or the tense of a verb. The phrase which defines the species 'man', if no verb in present, past, or future time be added, is not a proposition.

…

'We call those propositions single which indicate a single fact, or the conjunction of the parts of which results in unity: those propositions, on the other hand, are separate and many in number, which indicate many facts, or whose parts have no conjunction.

'Let us, moreover, consent to call a noun or a verb an expression only, and not a proposition, since it is not possible for a man to speak in this way when he is expressing something, in such a way as to make a statement, whether his utterance is an answer to a question or an act of his own initiation.

'To return: of propositions one kind is simple, i.e. that which asserts or denies something of something, the other composite, i.e. that which is compounded of simple propositions. A simple proposition is a statement, with meaning, as to the presence of something in a subject or its absence, in the present, past, or future, according to the divisions of time.'

In everyday thinking we are very casual about using propositions. One of the basic rules of an intelligent thinking is becoming aware that we are constantly proposing, often without any self-criticism that would ask: 'Am I certain that this proposition is true?' When I hear some gossip about someone who I don't like myself, it slips easily over to my own propositions. For example: 'Ian has been unfaithful to his wife.' Maybe that isn't true at all, but it is said about Ian, and it comes as a truth into the world.

A proposition is formed when a substance - as a subject - is bound to an accident (accident, as used in philosophy, is an attribute which may or may not belong to a subject, without affecting its essence) by a verb in the present tense: 'the woman stands in the garden.' 'The woman stood in the garden' is a weaker proposition; 'the woman will stand in the garden' gives no sure proposition at all.

In this week 'proposition' is the theme for our meditation. First (always after the preliminary exercises), we recall the theme of the previous week, when we became aware that simple words don't provide truth or untruth. Then we proceed to thinking about making true or false propositions. We can use the concepts that we have collected in recent weeks, the concepts of Lull and Aristotle to form propositions. So we can investigate the worth of a proposition. In fact, the lines we have drawn in the circle of nine concepts are already a kind of set of statements, but not allied to a subject outside those nine concepts. When I say: 'Goodness is great', it is still a form of evident proposition. It only becomes a real proposition when it is connected to a substance: 'Tom has a certain wisdom.' This proposition is vague, because we would have to ask: 'What kind of wisdom, where does it originate, what do we mean by: 'a kind of... '?' When we say: 'this table is made of mahogany', the proposition is uniform and clear. Here we can learn to perceive the difference between a full irrefutable truth and a vague proposition of which truth can hardly be admitted, without asking more questions.

Then we think about nine possible questions, in the way Ramon Lull formulated them:

Whether, what, out of which, why, what quantity, what quality, when, where, how.

After thinking about the phenomenon of propositions, forming a number of them and questioning them, we can move on to grasping the meaning of 'making a proposition', to understand it as a concept. We are skilled thinkers, so we can perform this transition from 'thinking *about*' to 'thinking *of*'.

We certainly will experience the propinquity to what we call a true or a false proposition. Here truth comes into our field of thinking, not as a concept but as a fact. We find it ourselves and will work it out next week.

Here is some more Aristotle to read – if we wish to:

'Thus, if it is true to say that a thing is white, it must necessarily be white; if the reverse proposition is true, it will of necessity not be white. Again, if it is white, the proposition stating that it is white was true; if it is not white, the proposition to the opposite effect was true. And if it is not white, the man who states that it is making a false statement; and if the man who states that it is white is making a false statement, it follows that it is not white. It may therefore be argued that it is necessary that affirmations or denials must be either true or false.'

This will be the meditation for the coming week.

The sixteenth week

We will meditate three fundamental logical principles over the coming three weeks. The first is the *Principle of the excluded contradiction*.

Aristotle formulated this principle: If a clear sentence gives a uniform proposition and it is possible to ask whether this proposition is true, then the proposition must be true *or* false and can never be true *and* false. The *fact* that is proposed in the sentence either *is* or *is not*. It can never be true and false at the same time.

Of course there are many sentences that are not in a shape such that we can say that the proposition is a fact that is true or false. If we say 'Napoleon was a good man', this sentence is not clear enough, it has too many possible meanings and is far too general to allow us to ask whether this proposition is true. But if we say: 'At this moment it is raining in Amsterdam' - then it is either true or it is not; although one could propose that only in a part of Amsterdam it is raining and in another part it is not. But for the given part it must be true or not true. Aristotle in his document '*On Interpretation*' provides many examples of propositions that can be true and untrue at the same time, for instance when something is said about the future (the fact may be true potentially, not actually).

In his own famous words:

> 'Let me illustrate. A sea-fight must either take place tomorrow or not, but it is not necessary that it should take place tomorrow, neither is it necessary that it should not take place, yet it is necessary that it either should or should not take place tomorrow. Since propositions correspond with facts, it is evident that when in future events there is a real alternative, and a potentiality in contrary directions, the corresponding affirmation and denial have the same character.

> 'This is the case with regard to that which is not always existent or not always nonexistent. One of the two propositions in such instances must be true and the other false, but we cannot say determinately that this or that is false, but must leave the alternative undecided. One may indeed be more likely to be true than the other, but it cannot be either actually true or actually false. It is therefore plain that it is not necessary that of an affirmation and a denial one should be true and the other false. For in the case of that which exists potentially, but not actually, the rule which applies to that which exists actually does not hold good. The case is rather as we have indicated.'

In the meditation we concentrate on the principle of truth first. Aristotle has in his logic given the 'rules' for finding the truth, beginning in the outer world. Here we mostly have to do with *facts* that are either true or not. But we have already thought this concept, and we know that truth is far richer than only related to the world of outer facts. When we want to state: 'God exists' - then it is quite another question whether this is true or not, compared to the case of the rain in Amsterdam. To get acquainted with the principle of irrefutable truth, however, it is best to follow Aristotle's uniform principles of truth.

When we have found the unspoken concept of truth, and have thought it also in an Aristotelian way, as we approached it during the past week, we can then concentrate on the principle of the excluded contradiction.

In his book '*Metaphysics*' Aristotle states that the rule of the excluded contradiction is the most certain principle of all principles. He finds it not sensible to deduce it from other principles. We have to accept this principle as a foundation of logic that we have to follow, whenever we want to prove something. If we cannot respect this principle we should stop thinking completely, for there would be no possibility of thinking and saying anything that makes sense. If it were possible that facts could at one and the same time be true and untrue, what would there be to think? Aristotle finds the desire to deduce this basic principle, as a sign of lack of education! If we are unable to accept that there is a beginning of all thinking, we would have to go back infinitely, attempting to prove what cannot be proved. (This is called an infinite regression).

In terms of Aristotle these kind of principles that cannot be based on other principles are called: axioms.

This basic principle, this axiom is what we have to investigate in this week. There are people who offend this rule in every sentence they speak. These are the weak thinkers, speaking on a weak foundation of truth.

But let us think now whether it is possible that this table here is made of mahogany and at the same time can be made not of mahogany. Can Tom have a certain wisdom and at the same time be a fool? Was Napoleon a good man and at the same time a bad person? Can goodness be great and small too? What kind of propositions follow this basic axiom?

After some fifteen minutes of clear thinking - we will have to 'force' ourselves to keep our mind clear and not to be distracted - we again try to perceive our thinking activity *as a fact that is true.*

The seventeenth week

The second principle of logic is '*Tertium non datur*', *the principle of the excluded third.*

Aristotle has formulated this principle also in his '*Metaphysics*'. A proposition that is capable of truth must be either true or untrue, there is nothing in between. From two contradictory propositions about the same fact, one has to be true and one has to be false. We must accept the one and then reject the other - there is no position in between through which it could be said that both are either true or false. (This is the main principle of our modern computer-programming). This principle also makes it possible to prove a fact as true by proving that the opposite is not true. This is called 'proof by contradiction'.

But the basis is that there have to be clear sentences that give uniform propositions, and that it is possible to ask whether the proposition is true or not.

Only an unclear thinking could not distinguish between the first and the second principle of logic. But our thinking has become clear now, and so we can clearly differentiate between principle one and principle two. That is our task now (having done the preliminary exercises).

1. Excluded contradiction

2. Excluded third.

In '*On Interpretation*' Aristotle works out in fine detail the several possibilities of propositions and judgments and their contraries. The full text can be found on the internet.

It would certainly sharpen our thinking if we exercised through reading this abstract text. But in these meditations we will not go so far. A first step is difficult enough. The considerations of Aristotle are, for instance: 'If we say: Socrates is wise ... what is the contrary of this judgment? Is It: Socrates is not wise? Or should it be: Socrates is unwise? Or even: Socrates is foolish?' We can try to feel the difference between the three contraries.

Only carry on reading Aristotle if you feel like it!

'Let me illustrate. There is a true judgement concerning that which is good, that it is good; another, a false judgement, that it is not good; and a third, which is distinct, that it is bad. Which of these two is contrary to the true? And if they are one and the same, which mode of expression forms the contrary?

'It is an error to suppose that judgements are to be defined as contrary in virtue of the fact that they have contrary subjects; for the judgement concerning a good thing, that it is good, and that concerning a bad thing, that it is bad, may be one and the same, and whether they are so or not, they both represent the truth. Yet the subjects here are contrary. But judgements are not contrary because they have contrary subjects, but because they are to the contrary effect.

...

'Now that which is good is both good and not bad. The first quality is part of its essence, the second accidental; for it is by accident that it is not bad. But if that true judgement is most really true, which concerns the subject's intrinsic nature, then that false judgement likewise is most really false, which concerns its intrinsic nature. Now the judgement that that is good is not good is a false judgement concerning its intrinsic nature, the judgement that it is bad is one concerning that which is accidental. Thus the judgement which denies the true judgement is more really false than that which positively asserts the presence of the contrary quality.'

So the most real contrary to the judgment 'Socrates is wise' is not 'Socrates is a fool', nor is it 'Socrates is unwise', but 'Socrates is not wise'. We should learn to perceive these differentiations and then go on to the principle of *tertium non datur*. If one person states: Socrates is wise and another person states the contrary, then one of these must be true and there is nothing in between. If we say: 'This table here is made of mahogany'; then the contrary is not: 'This table is made of oak'; but it is: 'This table is not made of mahogany'. If we contradict by saying that the (same) table is oaken, this certainly is another judgment, but it does not give not the contrary judgment.

Thus 'not good' is not the same as 'bad', 'not great' is not the same as 'small', 'not eternal' is not the same as 'temporary', 'no power' is not the same as 'weak', and so on.

'Physics is a quantitative science'. The contrary is not: 'Physics is a non-quantitative science'; or: 'Physics is a qualitative science'. The contrary is: 'Physics is not a quantitative science'. Is 'quantitative' the intrinsic nature of physics? If it is, this last contrary is the most real contrary. If not, the proposition is not uniform and the contrary also cannot be said to be perfectly clear and uniform. If we state that physics is a quantitative science because 'quantitative' is the true intrinsic nature of it, then the predicate 'not quantitative' is false, and there is no third possibility.

After thinking for about fifteen minutes, we try to perceive and feel the notion of this second principle. We will find that it lies as a foundation in our thinking, that it is like a faraway shadow - but now as it becomes clear, we draw it into the full light of our comprehensive thinking. And we repeat:

Thinking concepts without truth or untruth
Thinking propositions that are clear and uniform
Thinking the first logic principle: The excluded contradiction
Thinking the second logic principle: The excluded third.

Try to direct the thinking to regard the activity of thinking.

The eighteenth week

The third logic principle is the famous 'syllogism'. In a short form: 'For when A can be predicated from every B and B from every C, then A must be predicated by every C.' This is a logic form that all thinking people know without being conscious of it, and that all people can apply correctly - although it is also the source of all fallacies.

Aristotle in *Prior Analytics:*

'A syllogism is discourse in which, certain things being stated, something other than what is stated follows of necessity from their being so. I mean by the last phrase that they produce the consequence, and by this, that no further term is required from without in order to make the consequence necessary.

'I call that a perfect syllogism which needs nothing other than what has been stated to make plain what necessarily follows; a syllogism is imperfect, if it needs either one or more propositions, which are indeed the necessary consequences of the terms set down, but have not been expressly stated as premises.

'That one term should be included in another as in a whole is the same as for the other to be predicated of all of the first. And we say that one term is predicated of all of another, whenever no instance of the subject can be found of which the other term cannot be asserted: 'to be predicated of none' must be understood in the same way.

...

'After these distinctions we now state by what means, when, and how every syllogism is produced; subsequently we must speak of demonstration. Syllogism should be discussed before demonstration because syllogism is the general: the demonstration is a sort of syllogism, but not every syllogism is a demonstration.

'Whenever three terms are so related to one another that the last is contained (implicit) in the middle as in a whole, and the middle is either contained (implicit) in, or excluded from, the first as in or from a whole, the extremes must be connected by a perfect syllogism. I call that term middle which is itself contained in another and contains another in itself: in position also this comes in the middle. By extremes I mean both that term which is itself contained in another and that in which another is contained. If A is being said of all B, and B of all C, A must be said of all C: we have already explained what we mean by 'predicated of all', or 'said of all'. Similarly also, if A is being said of no B, and B of all C, it is necessary that no C will be A.'

The well-known formula is:

All human beings are mortal,
Socrates is a human being,
Socrates is mortal.

The conclusion is only true if the premises are true. If the premises are true and the way of logical conclusion is right, the conclusion is right.

Perfect syllogisms are self-evident statements which do not possess and do not need a demonstration. That was already stated as so by Aristotle. He gives four such syllogisms. Hav-

108

ing developed the art of thinking, we can now recognise deep within ourselves how these syllogisms are therefore evident, because they are fully our own; we don't have to learn them or become conscious of them to apply them perfectly - but the process of becoming conscious is really a wonderful experience, which we reach at this point.

Here are the four evident syllogisms.

- All M are A, all B are M. Conclusion: All B are A
All human beings are mortal, all Americans are human beings, so all Americans are mortal.

- No M is A, all B are M. Conclusion: No B is A
No human being is immortal, all Dutchmen are human beings, so no Dutchman is immortal.

- All M are A, Some B are M. Conclusion: Some B are A
All human beings are mortal, some beings are human, so some beings are mortal.

- No M is A, Some B are M. Conclusion: Some B are not A
No human being is immortal, some beings are human, so some beings are not immortal.

There are ten other forms of syllogisms that are not immediately evident. These I will not discuss here.

Our aversion to abstract thinking can become very strong here! Still, these are the most important forms of logic that there are, and they belong to the human being just as his erect position belongs to being human. Maybe it requires some self-discipline to dive into these four forms, but this is our last task. If we have come so far that we have exercised all the themes until now, this should be no problem - despite any strong waves of aversion. The point is to perceive our own logical thinking by thinking these four forms, to experience that there is, hidden deep in our mind, the existence of these forms, of logic itself. If we can feel this, it will reveal a wonderful self-knowledge, which is not given only to my Self, but to all human Selves that come so far that they can perceive and feel the wonder of thinking.

The nineteenth week

In this final week of the first round of meditations in the art of thinking, we have to play with thinking as if we were a musical soloist playing a virtuoso cadenza of variations on the theme of the concert. We can listen to a violin concerto of Brahms or Tchaikowsky or Mendelssohn or any classical concerto we want, and we will hear such 'virtuous' solo-playing. In this, we human beings reach a culmination of our human faculties. And this really is an outer performance equivalent to what thinking in the inner life of the mind can be, if we develop our thinking *to the level of an art*. In this book we have laid the foundation for this thinking as a human art. In following volumes this will be developed further, until we can feel like a soloist playing on our own instrument: Intelligence.

Aristotle gives us an example of pure thinking. But since his time, human thinking has developed and has become an instrument not only for science, but also for the development of instruments, machines that can do something that gives the impression of thinking. We can go back to Aristotle as if going back to our roots. But after that, the art of thinking can be developed in an almost endless way.

At the end of the preliminary exercises as set out in this book, in order to reach thinking as an art that gives us the power to live our life, that heals our mind and our body, we will have to play a cadenza. We have behind us eighteen weeks of content and movement of thinking. In the cadenza we will have to progress through all the themes in an original way of thinking. We think all that we have thought over the past eighteen weeks, but we have to do this in about fifteen minutes. We will discover a complex thinking that is neither complete nor perfect, of course, but that is a foundation.

So - we think the nine concepts of Lull and draw the lines as given in the first figure; we then think the ten categories of Aristotle and the elaborated category of relation as given by Lull in the third figure.

After that we think about *concepts* that are thought *without* a *proposition*, then about *proposition*, about *true* and *false* propositions, about the *two principles* of *logic* and about the *syllogism*. But we try to think, not as though we were storing all our thought-properties in folders and cabinets, nicely tagged so that we can call them up easily, or as if we might save them on the pc... On the contrary, we try to think them in an art-filled way, as if the heart would love them – or rather, not 'as if', *the heart does indeed love them and loves the producing, the movement, the feeling of truth and untruth, the feeling of the waves of activity that are full of meaning.*

After finishing this thought-expedition, we could turn around and think backwards, or in another sequence, we could try to harmonize the different concepts with the categories, and so on. Thus we learn to play an increasingly virtuosic cadenza.

It will become ever more clear that these thinking-exercises not only make thinking stronger and bring it under the mastery of the thinker, but also that they get ever closer to *a thinking that is truth in itself.* Actual thoughts form themselves from within as truths. Actual truth shines through the facts.

Retrospect and prospect

Thinking is the most colourless psychic action there is. Through meditation in the region of thinking it becomes more colourful every day. After nineteen weeks we may come to the conclusion that our thoughts are as colourless as they were before. But we should not expect to see red and green thoughts now! I mean that the thoughts become clearer, more differentiated, as white light is differentiated into the colours of the rainbow. It is the will in thinking, the commitment, the engagement that makes thinking stronger and nearer to truth.

While we have undertaken some preliminary exercises, what we have so far developed is certainly not yet the full art of thinking. We will need progressive studies to reach that. All the same, we have built a strong foundation for the art of thinking.

We have taken the nine concepts of the Spanish thinker Ramon Lull as a starting point. Some centuries earlier, there was a great academy of the seven free arts in Chartres, where we can still visit that masterpiece of religious art, Chartres cathedral. This Cathedral is a kind of stone book where we can read the contents of the seven free arts. These are founded on three arts and we will now discover that we have developed them ourselves.

The first art is the true and *right forming of concepts*, the building stones of intelligence. We exercised this over fourteen weeks. It is a forming of 'words' that are not yet to be used for propositions and judgments. The faculty of forming sentences with these words is already present, but we have chosen not to use it yet. Then, in the fifteenth week, we learned to know the art of the right proposition, *to form sentences* with concepts that state something. Here the first art graduates to the second art. And in exercising the principles and *rules of logic*, we graduated to the third art.

In Chartres the first art was called '*Grammar*'. The art of pure concepts and their coherence.

The second art was called '*Rhetoric*'. In fact it is the art of fair speaking. But in thinking, which comes prior to speaking, rhetoric is the art of thinking in pure, coherent and consistent thoughts.

The third art was called '*Dialectic*' or 'Logic'. In the Royal Portal of the cathedral of Chartres Aristotle represents this art; he is often called 'The dialectician'. And here we find pure logic in thinking, the principles of logic and the syllogism as the fundamental rule for coming to conclusions.

Together these three arts were called '*the Trivium*'.

In old forms of expression we could say that we have now reached a level of understanding of the status of 'baccalaureatus artes liberales'. This has become the modern university grade of 'bachelor of arts'. It is merely an understanding. We will have to complete more nineteen week courses, to achieve this degree in thinking. But even then we will still not have reached our aim!

We aspire to become 'master of arts', 'magister artes liberales' - or rather, do we want to become a 'magister' in the art of thinking? In about a year's time there will be a new volume of this meditative path, and the subject will be the more scientific side of the seven free arts:

Arithmetic as a meditation on the teachings in arithmetic of Pythagoras.
Geometry as a meditation on several well understood simple and complex figures.
Music in relation to the art of thinking.
Astronomy inspired by the thoughts about the planets and the fixed stars.
These four arts together were called '*the Quadrivium*'.

Perhaps we will need more than one volume to cover these themes!